I HAVE WRITTEN

MUSIC STRINGS

BY MAKIZ E WORTH

About The Author
Mary A Crawley aka Makiz E Worth

I grew up in Somerset, NJ, graduated from Franklin High School. I've been writing since I was 15.
In a gospel group along with four of my seven sister until I was twenty years old.
The mother of two and Nana of one, I am truly blessed.
I have worked in a number of fields in my life, none of which I was ever satisfied.
I Am A "POET" pure and simple....
Feeling alone in a family of 11 I found solace in my ability to instruct my pen
to express, sing, cry and bleed for me.
I remain grateful to God For The Journey He Has Set For Me....
My joy came in 2003 when I realized with help from loved ones that writing was truly my purpose.
"I sat on my source for over twenty years not being confident not facing my fears"
I have written new poetry, greeting cards, songs and three mini plays .copyrighted all that spilled from my pen....
I have never felt more productive in my life........

Acknowledgments

I Acknowledge;

All That have encouraged me.

All that have smiled at me.

All that have loved me.

All that have taught me.

All that have listened to me.

All that have helped me.

All that Preached the word of God.

All that share my bloodline.

All the Corna Poets

All Precious Promise Art Circle

All that have read my works.

All that have comforted me.

Most of all and not least he whom has answered my prayers

God......

Much Love To You All....Mary

Dedication

I dedicate my works to my family, Robert Sr, Aisha, Robert Jr, Nana's' Baby Nasere, all my sisters and brothers, Mary Lee, Georgia Lee, Lillie B, George III, Hanif, Andrew, Shelia, Jeanette, Debby, Valarie, my father George Foy Jr, my mother Clara Thompson, Grandmothers Bessie Key Foy and Mary A. Powell, Grandfathers George Foy Sr and Benjamin Thompson, nieces and nephews, cousins, aunts, uncles too numerous to name. God and all these people shaped me and without them I would not be who I am and exist in the manner that I do. I know they all have impacted my life in ways that can never be fully explained.

I am thankful!
1 luv Makiz

Biography

Mary A Crawley aka Makiz E Worth

I am Makiz E Worth: I am a member of Precious Promise Art Circle Of NJ and Sister Group The Traveling Poets. The Traveling Poets has performed at various functions over the years. The performances included appearances on Rutgers University Radio Station (New Dawn Productions) with Alvin Fair, Spook Handy' "Night Of 1,0000 Words. I Have also acted in a play at George Street Playhouse all in New Brunswick, NJ.

I have personally read and or sang at Martin L King, Father's Day, Mother's Day and Gospel Programs locally.   I have worked published in the New Brunswick Free Public Library Reference Area under Mary A Crawley (Yearly Anthology) 2003 – 2013 . 2015 will be the 8ᵗʰ entry. I have written 8 poetry books. I also Have a "Words Of Pause" (original quotes) book in draft form just waiting along with the others to be published. I have written and copyrighted (via L O C in Washington) over three hundred poems, 14 song lyrics, three mini plays, forty greeting cards and authored 80 original quotes.

"God Is Good" He just lead me to share my work in 2003....
I am so very grateful for the journey he has laid before me....

I HAVE WRITTEN

MUSIC STRINGS

BY MAKIZ E WORTH

"Poetry Is The Music Strings To Our Hearts The Words Are The Notes"

Poetry

A spiritual journey expressed in words. not necessarily directed to any specific person or persons and

sometimes it will. That is the beauty of "Spoken Word" only in the eye of the individual

person can there be a light shinned. Take some reflection, lesson or even dislike to it, doesn't really
matter because a
True Poet's Pen Is Gonna Love, Rain, Roar, Whisper, Inspire and Bleed ,Last but not by a long shot least, Pray Regardless.......

ARTIST DIRECTION

SWIRLS AND COLORS CURVES AND LINES
TRANSFORMED INTO WRITTING IT DOWN FAST OR
TAKING YOUR TIME

WAKING AT WEE HOURS OF THE NIGHT
NOT SLEEPING TIL YOU GOT IT RIGHT

HORROR, PAIN, LOVE AND TRUST SPILLING YOUR HEART
IS A MUST

COMES TO YOU IN A FLASH, LIVING YOUR FUTURE, TELLING
YOUR PAST

SOMEONE SAID TO ME THERE IS PRIDE IN SHARING YOUR BABIES WRITTEN
DOWN AND THEY ARE CORRECT I HAVE FOUND

I CAN CALL MYSELF AN ARTIST I AM PROUD TO SAY
MY DIRECTION IS CLEAR IVE FOUND MY WAY.......

Broken Window Pane

Feeling your heart beat in silence

The sunset pierces your eyes

Weeping is Oh! So one with the rain

Salvation retreats with ever step you take

Each star you see one by one burns your soul

Leaves that never wrestle the wind

Tears are obsolete now

*The window pain that helped you
see is shattered....*

You Can't Miss

We are all connected
our hearts splintered and affected

There's no trying when it comes to the word
it just flows like a soaring bird

Just relax and let the words in your hearts pulse move
into your mind to your hands down your pen you've got the groove

You've got what it takes I'm a witness
go for what you know
YOU CAN'T MISS!!!!!!!!!!!!!!!!

Check Your Morality

If you know then its a shame
that you would sweet talk, hurt & mame
another that feels so much a part of you
so very close confusing the two

You can't go around using and throwing away
people who love you
one day you'll have to answer above too

Now, if you understand then that's
something you can correct
If you've have been hurt too, that's cause
and effect

Get it together or you in the end will regret
you see
the destruction of the human spirit
Is Deception Of Your morality....

Eighteen Years C J
02/2001

C.J we have seen your son my god! it's
like looking at your face
we know he wonders why we invade his space

But it's not just that, it's his stance
his smile, his skin
he looks so much like you did back then

Arisa Oh! Arisa a woman now
she's so determined and we know how
your in her deep, loving, and strong
but C.J. oh! C.J. it's been so long

And Christin we wish we knew her we
always hear it, just more beauty left
by your wonderful spirit

Carter Jay Smith time has passed and we miss you still

Carter Jay Smith we always will....

Come On Home

Brilliant no doubt
ur ability to hold ones intellect
amazing THUS the invitation
is about
UR play on words are
what illuminates such FORM
leaving wasn't the idea
frankly it was OUT of the norm
CAUSE isn't this what were here for
to be delighted, stimulated
to no end RETURN, it will be welcomed
and surely not to offend
Diversity is the SPICE of writing
we all look for it in our READS
SO do what u DO follow my lead
One letter after the other til ur
MASTERPIECE is done looking beneath the
lines we see from whence u come
PEOPLE in glass houses SHALL
throw no stones, noone is guiltless
mon cheiri ; Come On Home............

Cryin Eye's

Someone told me I had crying eyes

what did they mean?

I pondered the idea over the years

Was it beacuase of the tears I shared
for babies in trouble

Maybe the emotion at the thought of people
not realizing the hurt they cause

Could it be the cry I do for my people

or the cry for my love ones, my children

Maybe the verses I write bleed tears all
over the paper

Does my pen cry when I write?

Does it all goes back to my crying eyes?

Did that person see inside my soul
through my cryin eyes?

Shall We Dance

Walked into the club
uneasy to be there
with a friend girl
shaky I swear

Sat at the bar
ordered a round of wine
to the ladies room I go
way back felt fine

Rounded the table halfway past
the length of the bar
my eyes caught anothers not very far

Directly ahead I saw him
captured me in his stare
glance held a second too long
I was his but not yet aware

I felt a sudden flutter
feeling very shy lowered my eyes
rounded the bar back to my seat
wondering why

Looked for him from then on
he also looked for me
spoken in a single glance
that's all it took
in his eyes the question lingered
Shall We Dance?

Words don't always hold true
the look in ones eye
can evoke a tell all trance
that knows the offer is

Shall We Dance?

Deception Of Reality
Love or Not

Does love make you rationalize
the irrational

Does love allow you to see roses when
all that is present is ragweed

Does love invoke rage that only
you understand

Does love enable you to feel the one you
love moods and fears

Does love make you wonder what
the other is doing at any given moment

Does love make you recognize
your own plight in every
love song you hear

Is love suppose to stress you,
worry you, cause you sleepless
nights, hurt you, anger you

I think not! Love or not!
Deception of your reality!

Deemed

I was deemed a bird in a guilted cage

I was deemed to be a prisoner in my own rest

I was deemed to mentally support carry and
raise one already reared

I was deemed to organize, to be the solver of problems

I was deemed a thinker, the remember
the care taker of another life & strength

I was deemed to endure a selfish, insecure,
worrisome kind of emotional fear that was nerved to be called love

Always fighting for space, creativity, breath and peace

My emotions always at its very ends

I was deemed; Then I was released

I was washed

I was full

I was breathing

I was feeling

I was freed.......

Distance

I wish I could forget the feelings you made me feel

*If only I could shake the ache in my heart and
pretend it's not real*

*If only when I see you, the pain wouldn't show in
my eyes*

If the words I love you!   were easier to say

*I wish we could share each other life instead of
looking from a distance*

Begin again with you for only an instance

*I pray to forget and forgive the love
I feel for you, and the times we spent just us two...*

Do For His Woman

Some men go from day to day

shucken and Jiven in everyway

There ain't no woman that doesn't need a man
to talk to her hold her hand

Some men use you for sex called love
some squeeze you tight as a glove

Some will love you to death
some will chase you til you're out of breath

Men sometimes do unnecessary
things to learn
they figure your love they have sincerely earned

Some men shower you with expensive things, but
they never think about that wedding ring

See! I know the best thing a man could do for
for me and for you
the best thing he can do
is be true !

Enough

When the world is not enough
to ease your pain

When the only person that can
make you whole calls your name

When the person you love most
has gone away

When your ready to be with them
this very day

When sorrow and grief are no longer present
with the thought of you not being here

When you realize that your quest
for peace is near

When the world is no longer enough!

Georgia Moon

What can I give to make it all okay

What can I do to keep you from hurting

What can I pull from the last of all I have

What words can be uttered to bring a miracle

What star can I catch falling

What moon can I watch til your well

*What sunset can I raise til it's high and
shinning on your face*

What wrongs can I right

What tears can I exchange with the rain

*What can make me understand why life chases
us towards pits, dark alleys, fears and
choices that lure us deep into our desires*

*What prayer can I echo from my heart and
soul*

Would life be life if we were never informed so

Would grass be green, the sky blue

Would love be the ultimate power...

What can I give to you? My Undying Love!!

Graceful Women

Women are the masterpieces of God
If they present themselves as Hoochies,
chickenheads, sluts, hoodrats or not....

It's only a matter of time before they realize their granduer
Princeses and Queens, Graceful, loving and pure.

In a effort to conform to the ideal imposed on them
of what they are expected to be they have temporarily
lost their way

All that you are as men is because of all that they
as women

All that you need is their loyalty and nurturing gifts

All that you do is because you need and want their attention
and caring

All that you want is love unconditionally and for them to be the
Queens they were meant to be

Thus so graceful and perfect for YOU!

I Can't Touch You

I see you but I can't touch you

I think of you but I can't linger on my thoughts

I feel you, but I can't want you

I think back but soon I can place you

I remember you but I can't really say you cared

I could have had you but I wouldn't give into you

I missed you for a while but it faded away

I think back again and then I do place you

I know you were in my life and then out

I dream but dreams seldom come true........

If We Could

If only I could reach out and
say I love you

If only I could hold you like
I'm longing to do

If only I could see through
all the falling stars

If only I could bring you closer
for you are so far

If only you could admit the
feelings you push down inside

If only you could push away
your foolish pride

If only we could be together
it's ashame it wasn't meant to be

If only love was fair instead
of causing misery.......

Injured

When ones soul has been injured
there's a void a void so very hard to fill

In an effort to do so, the wrong things are
pushed and pulled in only to further open
the wound

Even though we recognize this

Organize it in our minds

Direct it in our wishes

Develop a protective arm

Attach ourselves to others of the
same sort

Cry for them and comfort them

A part of our soul is looking to mend
still searching for its fill

We know all of this

We feel all of this

We rationalize all of this

Yet Our Soul Remain Injured...

Our Inspiration

Our inspiration is from a nation
pillaged and stolen away

Stripped of all they knew left a few
to struggle to find their way

We hail from kings and queens who
lived and loved on strength and pride

Only to be dehumanized; raped,
beaten& turned on each
other by good old Willie Lynch
"damn his hyde"

he culture was set out to be used
and then destroyed, that was the plan
but someone slow the process down
In it, came another hand

We over came, over achieved, over loved,
over time squashed their speed, moved ahead
with leaps and bounds then
pulled our courage from what we found

We were not suppose to survive the TRADE!
THE TEST! "Our Inspiration Came
From Nation" Of Them We Got The Best.......

Integrity

*The person who has it is the one concerned
about it*

*The person who has it smiles at perfect
strangers*

*The person who has it knows how precious
a child is*

*The person who has it gives of themselves
expecting nothing in return*

The person who has integrity

*The one who loves themselves first and
lets everything else fall into place*

INTEGRITY

We all have it we just have to exercise it

In The Mind Of Writers

A true writer holds in their mind
an array of words, phrases, scenes,
backgrounds, passion, love, anger,
sadness, fear, romance and music

Long walks, sleepless nights, discipline
and spiritual output....

A writers mind will experience
overbearing insight of all that he or
she sees, hears, knows and feels....

A writer will most times prophetically
astound you....

A writers mind......

Liquid Merging Of I

n ponds battle my mind
fighting for space, breath,
creativity ode to my rescue
of slumbering verses

In springs battle my heart
on my sleeve not aware of
whom may happen upon it

In lakes battle my spirit
where my emotions lie
high, drained and satisfied

In rivers battle my soul
open, vunerable, often
disabled, heavy yet full of vigor

In oceans battle my body
smooth, knowing, graceful, passionate
chancing delicately to pursue my
undeniable destination

In seas battle my liquid movement
connecting, emptying, into all that is
searching, engulfing, merging what
has sought the liquid measure of my being...

What Men Want

What our beautiful men want
is to use one idea to handle us all
the more they try the harder they fall

They sit around shooting the breeze
talking about how they handle their
women with ease

Men want to keep the myth alive
LET A MAN BE A MAN!

If a man is a man, on his own he
should be able to stand

Noone can let him be or not be you see
It's really quite simple, listen to me!

Where our brothers make there mistake
is lumping us together like were all fakes

Different women want different things
like specialist in a hospital we all have our own wings
we are individual, exact, separate yet connected
we all may have spots but were not all Leopards

Men want to call it
so in a neat box we fit

Never that my men, never that
we wear an aray of multicolor hats

So do the work handle your biz
it's just not that simple
nothing worth having is......

Music

The music has always charmed me
from the depth of my being watched over me

The music has always rocked me silently
luing me to sleep echoing in my inner most child
surrounding my heart keeping me sane
answering my prayers without speaking a word
yet breathing and whispering to me

The music lives in my mind, heart, arms, legs and feet
back to my finger tips

The music has sustained me nourishing
me like water 80% of my body

Music has made me whole, a woman
strong and intelligent

Music is Love
The Sweet Music Is Love.......

My Pain

When I live for my pain

I loose my ability to care

When I live for my pain
the sadness lives in my stare

When I live for my pain
misery is worn not overcome

When I live for my pain

I forget where it even came from

When I live for my pain

I can't feel past yesterday

When I live for my pain

Joy can't come my way

When I live for my pain

I fail the ultimate test of what my life should be

When I live for my pain

Peace & happiness look for me but can not see...

Obstacles

Sometimes God removes obstacles
from our path

So we can bring to ourselves what will fill us
up with joy

If the obstacles return

He keeps intervening until we see
his way

Remember your strength, your intelligence
your ability to survive with Gods help is in your hands

Heed his words and signs

You want better

You deserve better

Most of all remember to love yourself and the rest will fall
in place........

Ode To The Iceman

He opened me up
A flower of pain
I must admit felt good
He sank into my thoughts
Like no one really should

Pulled my power from inside out
Without a single touch
With his use of words
Clever no doubt
Til I hungered just as much

Needed me for a short time
Or did I need him
My heart and mind he did move
Was this just his whim

Can I believe what he spouts
Just cause he says so
Is he what he seems to be
I guess I'll never know

So far yet so close
But a stroke away
He saw me but I not he
I wonder ti this day

Could never face him
Said too much gone the distance
Gazing at the evening sky
I picture him just a instant

Back to his life
What ever it may be
Drifting back to his world
Back and he goes without......... Me

Okay My Brother !

Okay my brother!

We heard what you said

We listened attentively

Don't mess with our head

*No excuses about how you can't
try harder or do better*

*It will take much more then a rebut
letter*

*We know only god is perfect
that we women can see*

*But you speak in a vague way
tryin to charm cherries from our tree*

*You wish, you want, you try to be
all that we need unsuccessfully*

*Don't hem and haw about what should
be your life quest*

*Rise above all that rhetoric
and start out by being your best....*

Okay My Brother!!

ON BEING DISCRIMINATED AGAINST

*I COULD UNDERSTAND IF I LACK INTELLIGENCE, PERSONALITY,
PEOPLE SKILLS, LEADERSHIP QUALITY, ORGANIZATION OR SENSATIVITY*

*THESE THING I COULD WORK ON IMPROVING, BUT MY BLACKNESS
IS MY HERITAGE AND IS MINE FOREVER
I CAN'T CHANGE OR WORK ON IT NOR WOULD I WANT TO*

*TO BE PUNISHED OR HELD BACK FOR SOMETHING THAT WILL NEVER BE OTHER
THAN IT ISTHE ULTIMATE BLOW*

*IT'S LIKE SAYING A BIRD HAS WINGS SO CONDEM IT TO LAND
A FISH SWIMS SO PUT IT ON THE GROUND KNOWING WATER IS ITS PLACE OF
ORGIN*

*LIKE TELLING A CRIPPLE TO WALK WITH A PROMISE OF THE USE OF HIS LIMBS
LIKE TELLING A BLIND MAN TO READ A PASSAGE TO REGAIN HIS SIGHT*

*BEING A VICTIM OF RACISM IS LIKE CARRYING AROUND A WEIGHT ON YOUR BACK
TO HEAVY TO REMOVE, THE LONGER YOU CARRY IT THE WEAKER YOU GET
PHYSICALLY YOUR DRAINED, MENTALLY YOU ARE AT ODDS WITH YOURSELF*

*THINKING IS IT POSSIBLE THAT YOU ARE REALLY NOT WORTHY
YOU HAVE DREAM OF INFERIORITY
DREAMS OF ONE DAY BEING ACCEPTED ON YOUR OWN MERIT*

THE WORSE FEELING IN THE WORLD IS TO FEEL THE FEAR

THAT COMES WITH BEING MADE TO FEEL

*YOU ARE NOT GOOD ENOUGH TO HAVE A PLACE IN THIS WORLD!
RACISM DISCRIMINATION
IS
THE DESTRUCTION OF*

THE HUMAN SPIRIT

CAN NOT AND WILL NOT BE TOLERATED

Our Great Men

Men by far are the greatest creation of God
whether they present themselves as hustlers,
pimps, players, ballers, scrubs, or even drug dealers or not

Its only a matter of time before they realize their greatness
Princes, Kings noble and royal

In an effort to conform to the land of the devil they temporarily
have lost their way

All that we are as women
is because of all that they are as men

All that we need is their strength and courage

All that we do is because we really love them

All that we want is for them to be the Kings
they were meant to be

Thus so great and perfect for us.............

Our Ancestors Love

BEFORE YOU OR I AND BEFORE OUR MOTHERS
AND FATHERS BEFORE THEIRS AND THEIRS
AND THEIRS AND THEIRS

THEY SENT THEIR LOVE TO US THRU THEIR
HEARTS AND SOULS, THE CLOUDS, THE MOON
THE SUN AND STARS

THEY UTTERED; "LONG AFTER WE HAVE
DEPARTED THIS LAND OUR BABIES, THEIR
BABIES AND THEIR BABIES AFTER AND AFTER
AND ON AND ON WILL GO FAR"

"LET US SEND THEM THE VERY BEST OF ALL
WE HAVE, THE STRONGEST THE BRIGHTEST TO
CONTINUE THE STRUGGLE, TO LEAD OUR
SPIRITS TO OUR BABIES HEARTS"

THEN IT WAS SPOKEN TO THEM WHO
INHABITED THE MOTHERLAND LONG LONG AGO
SO SHAKA KING OF THE ZULUS, NEHANDA OF
ZIMBABWE, NANDI QUEEN OF ZULULAND, HATSHEPSUT THE ABLEST QUEEN,
TEKAMENIN KING OF GHANA, JAI KING OF
OPUBO, AKHENATON PHAROH OF EGYPT, MAKEDA QUEEN OF SHEBA,
SET FORTH A WAVE OF CONCERNMENT TO DO THEIR PART

THEY SENT TO US HARRIET T, FREDRICK D. SOJOUNIER T,
NAT T, LANGSTON H, RICHARD W, GEORGE C, THURGOOD M,
W.E.B D,MANDAME CJ W, JESSIE O, MANDELLA, JACKIE R,LOUIS F, ELIJAH M,
MARTIN L. K, MALCOM X,
ANDREW Y, TIGHER W, AND COLON P TOO
WHAT WERE OR ANCESTORS TO DO"?

WE GRASPED THE LOVE AND HELD IT TIGHT IN OUR HANDS,
BUILT OFF THE HURT, SWEAT, TEARS, AND SHAME, THEN REPLACED IT
WITH LOVE, FAITH AND HOPE...

Promised

Father you are my first love

Father my source of male strength

*Father I smile like the sun when
I see you coming*

*Father I looking your eyes for
approval*

*Father when you hold me I am safe
and secure*

*Father I will ever hear your words
of advice*

Father you make me whole

*Father I saw you love and respect
my mother*

*Father always steadfast, dependable
courageous and true*

*Father its not what you are but
what you do*

*Father I will always need and want
your love*

*Father without saying a word
you promised......*

RELATIONSHIPS

RELATIONSHIPS GOOD AND BAD
REMEMBERING THE GOOD TIMES YOU ONCE HAD

LOVE SHOULD BE INVOLDED IT'S NOT
ALWAYS THE CASE

AND WHEN IT'S ALL OVER YOU FEEL IT WAS
A WASTE

RELATIONSHIP SHOULD BE
GOOD FOR YOU, NOT BAD FOR ME

START OUT WITH RESPECT, TRUST
AND FRIENDSHIP THAT WILL BE
YOUR BASE

SO YOUR RELATIONSHIP WON'T BLOW
UP IN YOUR FACE...

Rose

Sometimes I feel as though I've passed
through a door
into a world that is not mine

A rose among wildflowers,

The times I looked to go back through
the door was closed

I've seen things, I felt things,
I've learned things on this side,

Now the door is a jar and it's waiting
for my return

I almost don't want to go back

But I know I have to and soon

If I don't the door will close

And the rose will be left on this side

among the wildflowers

She Knows

She knows how beautiful she is
She just doesn't act like she does

She knows its been along time without her true love
She knows who it is, it's she

She lives with his lies and his crazy lustful
need to posses her She knows who he is, it's he

She confuses love with a feeling she knows is
overwhelming
She knows he represents all that is lost inside
of her she can't yet tear herself away

She knows if she loved herself more there
would be no need to keep up the facade
that tells her she loves and needs him...

She knows who she is, it's herself

ITS SHE

My Sister My Friend

My sister My friend
I am your friend
You are my friend
We are friends

Grandness always in your heart
looking high above the horizon
wondering what's further than your reach
Chasing life, right on its heels
Refusing to settle for less

Your curiosity and eagerness will take you far
I miss you already

My prayer for you is guidance to find your way
Your heart to know happiness
Peace to find love

My sister My friend
I am your friend
You are my friend
We are friends..

So Flip Super Fool

Sleep all day walk the streets all night
trying to get over with out effort or fight

Trying to pounce on the weakest prey
knocking every positive force out of his way

Try once, try twice hell soon succeed
because he's as smooth talking ashe is mean

So super kool makes him a super fool
so super fine, not all the time
just at night
when he's feeling right

So super obvious

So super stupid

He's full of I deals but none of them are real

So very aware of his actions before he performs them

So super noticeable every body knows him....

Tell Her

How can I tell her
that she's making a mistake
tell her, the man is a fake

How can I say the words that are so hard to say
tell her she doing it the wrong way

Tell her he's selfish, mean
tell her only on the surface does he seem clean

Tell her, I know him better than she ever will
tell her, he's involved with someone else still

Tell her there's so much I know
tell her when she loves him so

Tell her to him woman are all the same

How can I tell her, because she'll eventually blame me
no one wants to hear that about their man you see...

Truth

Truth will set you free, believe me

Truth will set you free, wait and see

Truth will set you free, try it out

Truth will set you free, tell you what it is all about

Truth will set you free, put your mind at ease

Truth will set you free, bring a liar to his knees

Truth will set you free, feel good about yourself

Truth will set you free, be truthful with everyone else

Truth will set you free...

Why Again

Why do you feel like you feel

Why do you hold on to me still

Why do you call me every day

Why are there certain things you will not say

Why when I question you, you say maybe

Why do you call me baby

Why do when its time to say goodbye

do I feel like I want to cry

Why when you kiss me does it mess with my mind

Why does these feelings feel so strong

and sincere capturing my attention and

make me love you my dear...

Writer Writes

The emotion writing brings of
the most personal intimate things

The feel of the pen in your hand
can take you over seas to another land

Love over flowing when you enter the realm
gives the writer the power standing at the realm

A writer writes because of the most
basic need you see

A writer writes to be literally in control and spiritually free.....

Jeanette;
10/06

It's early Sunday morning
I just want to say
you're the best of the best
on your special day

Though I have always known this
your heart oh so kind
it makes it oh so blessit
when it'a at a magical time

You give your all to
everyone you see
love truth and understanding
you even listen to me

grateful to have a bestie
that happens to be family
God has truly blessed me
with you, see....

Happy Birthday My Sistah Gurlfriend...
Have A Glorious Day...

I Just Wanted To Share A Quote I Wrote;
Be Inspired, I Was......Sometimes I write Words And Read Them Later And Can't Believe It
Came From Me.....Like When My Children Were Born And I Use To Look At Them In Awe
And Could Not Fathom That These Beautiful Precious Little Beings Could Have Come
From Me, Of Me....The Same With My Grand....WOW!!!!.. ? Does This Just Mean God Is
At

Work The Things We Stand In Awe Of.....I Will Have To Assume Yes.......Thus; Answering
My Own Question...

"when fear is looking you in your face stare it down, when sadness fills your heart empty it
out, when love looks for you be still, when joy comes your way shine your light, when God
speaks to you be sure to listen; for the test above is not a multiple choice.."

-org quote..Makiz

I HAVE WRITTEN

MUSIC STRINGS

By Makiz E Worth

PRINTED IN THE USA
2013

www.ingramcontent.com/pod-product-compliance
Lightning Source LLC
Chambersburg PA
CBHW081617170526
45166CB00009B/3001